D1483122

# GOBLIN SHARKS

ELIZABETH THOMAS

Published in the United States of America by Cherry Lake Publishing
Ann Arbor, Michigan
www.cherrylakepublishing.com

Consultants: Dominique A. Didier, PhD, Associate Professor, Department of Biology, Millersville
University; Marla Conn, ReadAbility, Inc.
Editorial direction: Red Line Editorial
Book design and illustration: Sleeping Bear Press

Photo Credits: SeaPics.com, cover, 1, 9, 11, 13, 17, 21, 23, 29; Wikipedia Commons, 5; Sleeping Bear Press, 7;
Mogens Trolle/Shutterstock Images, 12; Dorling Kindersley RF/Thinkstock, 15; Aleksandrs Marinicevs/
Shutterstock Images, 18; Dray van Beeck/Shutterstock Images, 24; Shutterstock Images, 27

Copyright ©2014 by Cherry Lake Publishing
All rights reserved. No part of this book may be reproduced or utilized in
any form or by any means without written permission from the publisher.

Library of Congress Cataloging-in-Publication Data
Thomas, Elizabeth.
Goblin sharks / Elizabeth Thomas.
    p. cm. — (Exploring our oceans)
  Audience: 008.
  Audience: Grades 4 to 6.
  Includes index.
  ISBN 978-1-62431-406-3 (hardcover) — ISBN 978-1-62431-482-7 (pbk.) — ISBN 978-1-62431-444-5 (pdf)
  — ISBN 978-1-62431-520-6 (ebook)
  1. Goblin shark—Juvenile literature. I. Title.

  QL638.95.M58T46 2014
  597.3—dc23                              2013006181

Cherry Lake Publishing would like to acknowledge the work of
The Partnership for 21st Century Skills. Please visit *www.p21.org*
for more information.

Printed in the United States of America
Corporate Graphics Inc.
July 2013
CLFA11

## ABOUT THE AUTHOR

Elizabeth Thomas is the author of several books for children. She received her master of fine arts in
Writing for Children and Young Adults from Hamline University. Currently, she lives on Cape Cod
in Massachusetts.

# TABLE OF CONTENTS

# CHAPTER 1

# A TERRIFYING CREATURE

In 1897, a Japanese fisherman caught an unusual creature. It was eventually taken to the United States, where it was identified. No fish like it had been found before. The species was a shark. It was given the name *Mitsukurina owstoni*. But the Japanese fishermen who caught the shark gave it a more fitting nickname: goblin shark.

More than 100 years later, divers were floating in the dark ocean. They were waiting to film the elusive goblin shark. Finally, the strange fish swam slowly into view.

*The goblin shark was thought to be quite strange when it was first discovered.*

## LOOK AGAIN

*Look at this photograph. What other creatures does it remind you of? How does the shark differ from other sharks you have seen?*

It looked as if it was alive when dinosaurs lived. It had a clumsy, flabby body. It had a pale pink color and a very long snout.

The shark swam away from the camera. The bizarre fish bumped into a diver's protected arm. The shark's mouth snapped open as quick as a lightning bolt. Its jaw unhinged and what looked like a second mouth thrust forward. It looked as if another fish had sprung from inside the shark's mouth. Rows of thin, sharp teeth latched onto the diver's wet suit. The goblin shark struggled to free itself as the camera recorded the mysterious creature.

The goblin shark is one of the oddest sharks in the world. It lives in **temperate** waters. Goblin sharks are found in the Atlantic Ocean off the coasts of Africa, France, and Portugal. They live in the western Pacific Ocean near Japan, Australia, and New Zealand. They are also found in the Indian Ocean near South Africa and Mozambique. Recently, goblin sharks have been found living off the

# RANGE MAP

RANGE OF GOBLIN SHARK

*Goblin sharks are found in only a few areas in the oceans.*

coast of California, near San Clemente Island. They have also been discovered living in the northern Gulf of Mexico just south of the Mississippi River. Goblin sharks live in the deep, dark parts of these oceans. They swim at depths of around 130 to 4,265 feet (40–1,300 m).

Much is still unknown about the goblin shark. Sightings of goblin sharks are rare. The depths at which they live may be part of the reason. Scientists and researchers continue to explore the deep ocean, hoping to learn more about goblin sharks. ◣

*Goblin sharks often swim in deep, dark oceans.*

# Not a Typical Shark

When people think of a shark, they often think of the great white shark. They might imagine a creature with a huge mouth and lots of large teeth. They might picture a dorsal fin on the shark's back poking above the water to announce its presence. The goblin shark does not look like this. It has even been called the "ugliest living shark." Some people have said the shark looks deformed. They have even said it looks like an alien.

One of the most noticeable features of the goblin shark is its long, flat snout. It is shaped like a **trowel**.

[ 21ST CENTURY SKILLS LIBRARY ]

This type of snout is unusual. But a couple other sharks have this type of snout as well. The long snout has many sensory organs that are used to detect prey. The goblin shark's nostrils are located at the base of its snout at each end of its mouth.

*When the jaw juts forward, the goblin shark looks like a fierce predator.*

Another main feature of the goblin shark is its unique jaw. When the shark attacks its prey, its jaw unhinges. Part of its jaw juts forward from inside the mouth. The shark almost looks like a different creature when its jaw juts forward. The jaw is lined with jagged rows of long, sharp teeth.

Many other sharks have sleek, streamlined bodies. The goblin shark does not. Its body is soft and flabby. Scientists have an idea why goblin sharks have loose, non-muscular bodies. It may be because goblin sharks don't have to swim constantly to find their prey.

*Many sharks, such as the great white shark, are sleeker and more powerful than the goblin shark.*

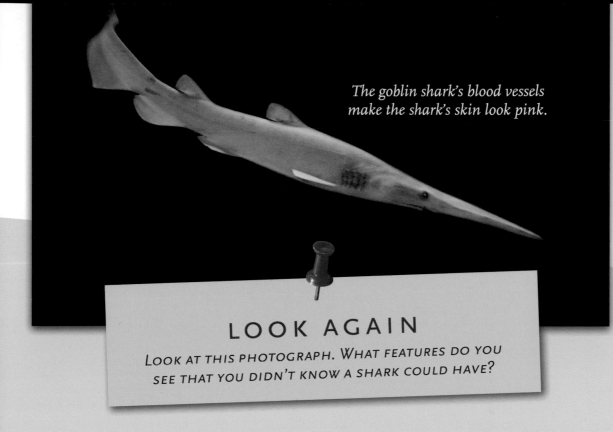

*The goblin shark's blood vessels make the shark's skin look pink.*

## LOOK AGAIN

LOOK AT THIS PHOTOGRAPH. WHAT FEATURES DO YOU SEE THAT YOU DIDN'T KNOW A SHARK COULD HAVE?

The goblin shark is also a different color than most sharks. Many other sharks are gray. Goblin sharks are light pink. This is because their skin is **translucent**. The blood vessels below the skin make the skin look pink.

The goblin shark lives in the deep ocean where light barely reaches. Therefore, it does not need large eyes. Its tiny eyes do not have **retractable** eyelids, as many sharks do. Like most sharks, the goblin shark's eyes have irises. The iris is the part of the eye that controls how much light gets into the eye. Having an iris means the goblin shark's eyes are sensitive to any light. A fish or squid that lights up near a goblin shark may become prey.

The goblin shark uses its gills for breathing, as other fish do. Water enters the shark's mouth and passes over the gills. The gills take oxygen from the water. The water then moves out through the gill slits. These are behind the goblin shark's mouth.

Another feature that sets the goblin shark apart from other sharks is its fins. They are not pointed like most sharks' fins. Instead they are rounded. The goblin shark's fins on the lower half of its body are usually larger than its dorsal fins. The goblin shark is not a fast swimmer. Its body shape and large fins are typical of a shark that swims slowly near the ocean floor.

Goblin sharks have several traits that help them stay afloat in the water. Their skeletons are made of **cartilage**. This is a lightweight, flexible material that is lighter than bone. Cartilage is the same tissue that makes up a human ear.

# BODY DIAGRAM

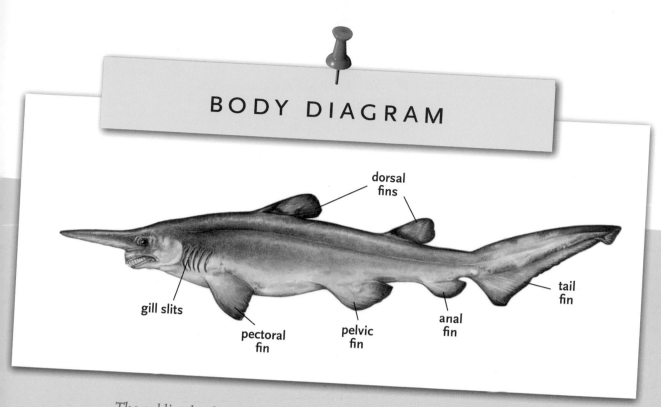

dorsal
fins

tail
fin

gill slits

anal
fin

pectoral
fin

pelvic
fin

*The goblin shark's body is not as streamlined as other sharks' bodies.*

Goblin sharks' large livers also keep them from sinking. A goblin shark's liver can be as much as 25 percent of the shark's weight. The liver is filled with oil. The oil is lighter than water. This makes the shark lighter and lets it swim in the water more easily.

Male goblin sharks range from 8 to 12 feet (2.4–3.7 m) long. Females are usually between 11 and 12 feet (3.4–3.7 m) long. ◢

# HUNTING AND EATING

Goblin sharks do not eat the variety of foods that many other sharks eat. Goblin sharks live in deeper waters than most other sharks. The deep ocean has fewer prey. Goblin sharks are limited to eating the species of animals that live in their **habitat**. Goblin sharks have been known to eat deep-sea rockfish, squid, crabs, and shrimp.

The goblin shark has not been observed hunting. Scientists have been able to put together ideas of how the shark hunts and eats from the way it looks. Other sharks are fast, powerful swimmers. Their coloring does a good job of hiding them so they can sneak up on their prey before they attack. Other sharks have thick skin, which protects them from prey that fights back.

*When the goblin shark bites prey, its jaw juts out and toward the creature.*

Goblin sharks eat squid
in the deep ocean.

## THINK ABOUT IT

*How are the feeding habits of the goblin shark different from other sharks? In what ways does this surprise you?*

In contrast, the goblin shark's flabby body and large, broad fins seem to mean the shark does not chase prey. Its thin skin could mean the goblin shark doesn't need protection from its prey either. The goblin shark floats well. Scientists think the goblin shark may hang motionless in the dark water. It lets its prey come to it. This would mean the goblin shark does not constantly swim to seek out prey the way many sharks do.

The goblin shark lives in the darkest parts of the ocean. This means it probably does not use its eyesight as its main way to find food. The goblin shark has a good sense of smell, as do most sharks. The shark is able to locate prey using its nostrils as guides.

The goblin shark also has a sixth sense called **electroreception** that many other sharks also have. This ability helps it locate food. The goblin shark's long snout is dotted with many sensitive organs called ampullae of Lorenzini. These sense organs detect the electrical fields created by the motion of other sea creatures. The ampullae of Lorenzini can detect a motion as small as the blink of an eye. These organs can even detect a heartbeat.

When prey gets close enough, the goblin shark thrusts its jaws forward. It seizes the prey with its jagged rows of sharp, slender teeth. Then the prey is pushed to the back of its mouth. The prey is crushed by the back teeth and then swallowed. Like most sharks, the goblin shark does not chew its food. ◢

*The goblin shark uses electroreception to find prey.*

# CHAPTER 4

# LIFE CYCLE

Little is known about the life cycle of goblin sharks. No studies have been done on their behavior in the wild. The very few goblin sharks that have been captured alive have lived for only a few days. Most information known about goblin sharks has been gathered from sharks caught accidentally in fishing nets. Scientists do not have much information about mating or pregnancy. They also don't know the number of **pups** born in a litter.

However, scientists have been able to make some educated guesses about behavior and the life cycle.

Several female goblin sharks have been recorded visiting the east coast of Honshu, Japan, during spring. Scientists wonder if the area is a breeding ground.

*Scientists think goblin sharks may go to special breeding grounds.*

*By studying the habits of other sharks, such as the blue shark, scientists can make educated guesses about the goblin shark's life cycle.*

[ 21ST CENTURY SKILLS LIBRARY ]

Scientists also believe goblin shark babies start inside the mother as eggs. Then the eggs hatch while the baby sharks are still in the mother. Scientists believe a goblin shark delivers live pups. This is similar to many other types of sharks. Most other shark pups take care of themselves the moment they are born. Scientists think goblin shark pups are able to live on their own right away as well.

Scientists do not know at what age goblin sharks can start having babies. Scientists also don't know how long goblin sharks live. Researchers continue to study the deep ocean. They hope to discover more about the mysterious life cycle of the goblin shark.

## GO DEEPER

*WHAT IS THE MAIN IDEA OF THIS CHAPTER? PROVIDE TWO PIECES OF EVIDENCE THAT SUPPORT YOUR CLAIM.*

# THREATS

Scientists do not think goblin sharks are the vicious predators imagined when one thinks of sharks like the bull shark. Still, researchers believe the sharks are **apex** predators in the deep ocean. This means they are near the top of the food chain and have few predators. Goblin sharks' biggest threat might be caused by humans. Occasionally, goblin sharks get caught in fishermen's nets and die.

Very little is known about the global population of goblin sharks. Scientists do not know how many there are.

Goblin sharks may be accidentally caught by
fishermen who are catching other fish.

They do not know how the population has increased or decreased over the years. This may be one reason goblin sharks do not appear on any lists of threatened species. The International Union for Conservation of Nature (IUCN) lists the goblin shark as a species of Least Concern on its Red List of Threatened Species.

Goblin sharks look like fish from prehistoric times. For a while, they were actually thought to be **extinct**. They live in deep waters and are rarely seen. Because of this, many things about their lives are still not known. Researchers continue to search for goblin sharks to learn answers to the many questions that remain about this unusual species. ◤

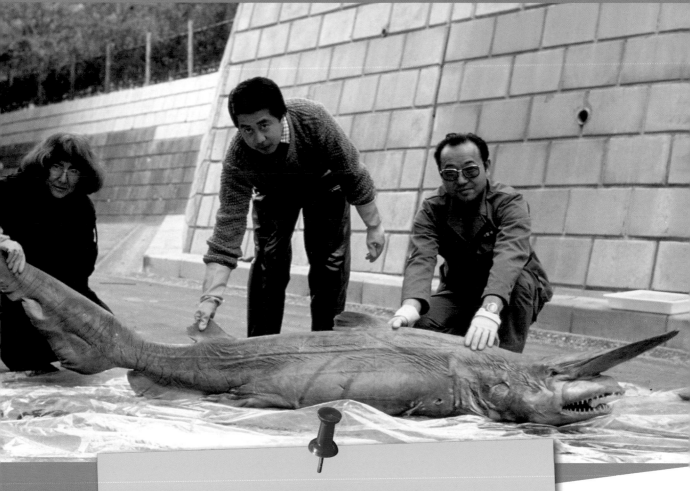

*Researchers continue to study goblin sharks
to learn more about their behavior.*

## LOOK AGAIN

LOOK AT THE PHOTOGRAPH. WHAT IS THE MOST
INTERESTING THING RELATING TO THE GOBLIN SHARK THAT
YOU SEE? WHAT SURPRISES YOU ABOUT THIS IMAGE?

# THINK ABOUT IT

▲ What was the most interesting fact you learned about the goblin shark? Is there more you would like to know? Read about goblin sharks on an informative Web site. How does the information compare to what you have learned from this book?

▲ Read Chapter 2 again. Compare and contrast the similarities and differences of goblin sharks with other kinds of sharks. What do you think is the most unique trait of the goblin shark?

▲ Review Chapter 4. What is the main idea discussed? List two pieces of evidence that support the main idea.

▲ In Chapter 5, you read that the goblin shark is not listed on endangered lists. What do you think would need to happen for it to be included on these lists?

# LEARN MORE

## BOOKS

Marsico, Katie. *Sharks*. New York: Scholastic, 2011.

Musgrave, Ruth. *Everything Sharks*. Washington, DC: National Geographic, 2011.

Smith, Miranda. *Sharks*. New York: Kingfisher, 2008.

## WEB SITES

### Discovery Kids—Sharks
http://kids.discovery.com/gaming/shark-week

This Web site lets readers play games and learn about shark attack survivals.

### National Geographic—Sharks
http://animals.nationalgeographic.com/animals/sharks

Readers discover different species of sharks, learn more about the ocean, and play games at this Web site.

## GLOSSARY

**apex (AY-pex)** at the very top

**cartilage (KAHR-tuh-lij)** a hard, flexible tissue that forms certain parts of animals' bodies, such as a human ear or a shark's skeleton

**electroreception (i-lek-tro-ri-SEP-shuhn)** a type of sense that allows sharks to detect the heartbeats of their prey

**extinct (ik-STINGKT)** no longer found alive

**habitat (HAB-i-tat)** the place where an animal or plant usually lives

**pup (PUP)** a baby shark

**retractable (ri-TRAK-tuh-bul)** able to be pulled back in

**temperate (TEM-pur-it)** not extremely hot or cold

**translucent (trans-LOO-suhnt)** not completely clear but lets some light through

**trowel (TROU-uhl)** a hand tool with a flat, triangular blade

## INDEX

3 1333 04641 6176